HORSES

HORSES

CHARTWELL
BOOKS, INC.

Published by Chartwell Books
A Division of Book Sales Inc.
114 Northfield Avenue
Edison, New Jersey 08837
USA

0-7858-0966-X

This book is produced by
Quantum Books Ltd
6 Blundell Street
London N7 9BH

Project Manager: Rebecca Kingsley
Project Editor: Judith Millidge
Design/Editorial: David Manson
Andy McColm, Maggie Manson

The material in this publication previously appeared in
The Illustrated Encyclopedia of Horse Breeds,
The New Book of the Horse,
Horse Facts

QUMSPHS
Set in Futura
Reproduced in Singapore by United Graphic Ltd
Printed in Singapore by Star Standard Industries (Pte) Ltd

Contents

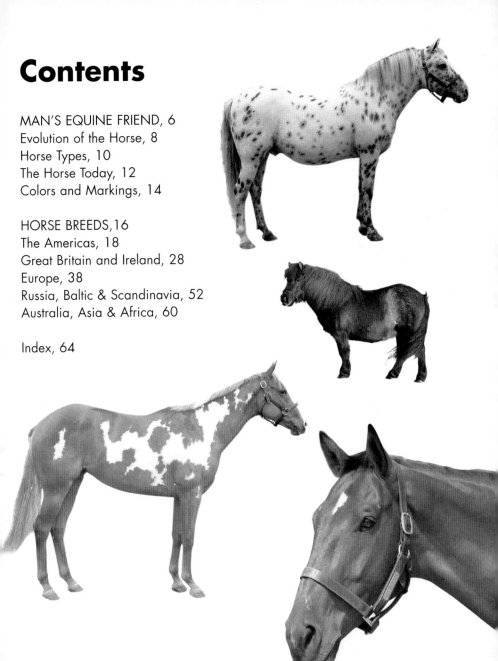

MAN'S EQUINE FRIEND, 6
Evolution of the Horse, 8
Horse Types, 10
The Horse Today, 12
Colors and Markings, 14

HORSE BREEDS,16
The Americas, 18
Great Britain and Ireland, 28
Europe, 38
Russia, Baltic & Scandinavia, 52
Australia, Asia & Africa, 60

Index, 64

MAN'S EQUINE FRIEND

The horse's original habitat of steppes and grassy plains provided little or no cover from predators, so their instinct to run at the first sign of danger developed as a defense. This instinct for flight has changed little through 5,000 years of domestication and is the natural basis for their supreme sporting activities today.

Evolution of the Horse

All present-day strains and types of horse and pony descend from the original wild ones which evolved, like other animals, by natural selection.

EARLY EQUINE ANCESTORS

The horse developed from a fox-sized creature called Eohippus which existed around 50 million years ago. This small mammal walked on pads like a dog which were well suited to the soft wet ground of the swampy forests in which it lived. It had four toes on the forefeet and three on the hind, each ending in a little rounded nail or hoof.

THE RUNNING INSTINCT

As the Earth's climate changed, different species of animal and vegetation evolved. Between 26 million and 7 million years ago, grassy plains developed across the American and Eurasian continents. Eohippus gave way to Parahippus, a larger grazing animal with a longer neck and head. It had longer legs and fewer toes on its feet to help it outrun predators on the grassy plains.

Eohippus, also known as Hyracotherium, is one of the earliest equine ancestors.

THE MODERN HORSE

The first one-toed ancestor, Pliohippus appeared between 7 and 3 million years ago. The foot and leg had altered and had become supported by a spring system of tendons and ligaments. Pliohippus was the immediate forerunner of Equus – the modern horse.

Equus, which includes donkeys and zebras, appeared about 1 million years ago. The ultimate specialist in running speed had arrived and was well established on Earth half a million years before man's arrival.

The zebra is one of the horse's closest relatives, also descended from Equus. It displays many features of primitive pony types, such as the upright mane and stocky body.

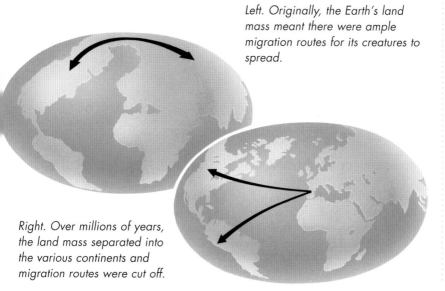

Left. Originally, the Earth's land mass meant there were ample migration routes for its creatures to spread.

Right. Over millions of years, the land mass separated into the various continents and migration routes were cut off.

Horse Types

There is considerable difference of opinion on the recent development of the horse. The most common view is that at the end of the last Ice Age, roughly 10,000 years ago, there were three main types of horse and pony.

PRIMITIVE HORSE TYPES

1. Forest Horse. Probably the ancestor of all modern heavy horses. It was slow moving and heavily built with broad heavy feet adapted for its marshy European habitat.

2. Asiatic Horse. Still exists today and is also known as Przewalski's Horse after the Polish explorer who discovered it in 1879.

3. Tarpan. Originating from Eastern Europe and the Southern Steppes of Russia. Its light build and speed suggest that many of our pony and light horse breeds descend from the Tarpan.

FOUR DIRECT DESCENDANTS

Around 5,000 to 6,000 years ago the three primitive types had produced four variants — two northern pony types and two southern horse types.

Pony Type 1. Lived in North West Europe and was small, chunky, tough and resistant to cold, wet windy weather. Today, the Exmoor Pony and Icelandic are similar types.

Pony Type 2. Living in Northern Europe this type was very resistant to sub-zero temperatures. Its closest modern-day relative is believed to be the Norwegian Fjord.

Horse Type 3. The tall desert/steppe horse of Central Asia had a great resistance to drought and heat. Its closest ancestor today is the Akhal-Teké.

Horse Type 4. This was a smaller desert horse from Western Asia. The modern Caspian could be a direct descendant.

HOT, WARM AND COLDBLOOD

Whether a horse breed is hot, warm or cold blooded is decided by its physical characteristics.

Cold blood. Suited to cold climates and built to retain body heat with rounder bodies and thicker coats.

Warm blood. Horses such as the Hanoverian and the Selle Français are crosses between hot blooded and cold blooded horses.

Hot blood. Horses and ponies from hot climates have finer hair, longer legs and carry their tails away from the body to facilitate heat loss.

The Horse Today

Since it was domesticated, the horse has been used for all types of work. Even today, every horse is, in practice, working for its living, whether it is a child's pony, a racehorse, show jumper or brewery dray.

THE WORKING HORSE

In the Western world, some breweries use heavy horses for short-haul deliveries and publicity purposes. Some farms still use heavy breeds and horses are an essential asset to the police in many countries.

However, throughout Eastern Europe, South America, Asia and Africa, working horses (including donkeys and burros) are still in widespread use for transportation and agriculture.

Left. A team of English brewery drays.

Above. The modern horse excels at show-jumping

THE SPORTING HORSE

The main role of the horse in the West today is in pleasure and sport. Equestrian sports go from strength to strength, and are increasingly popular with both riders and spectators.

Hunting and polo are both ancient sports, while horse racing has been popular around the world since the early 18th century.

Many forms of equine competition involve large sums of money, both paid for and won by horses as well as sponsorship deals.

However, the main attraction for the public lies in watching the superb achievements and courageous performances of the horse which have made it the object of man's admiration and affection over the centuries.

Colors and Markings

The horse's coat insulates the body against extremes of temperature and the effects of the elements. It is water resistant and varies in texture according to the horse's genes and habitat.

COAT COLORS

Breeds which evolved in cold regions for example, often have virtually waterproof coats with a soft underlayer for extra insulation. Within color categories there are different shades and varieties. Some of the most common are shown on the facing page.

FACIAL MARKINGS

Facial markings are an important means of identification. Some of the common ones are shown below.

HEIGHT BOXES

Throughout the book, height boxes are used to display the height range for each particular breed in hands.

16hh

MAPS

The country of origin of each horse is shown on the small map in each entry.

White face

Snip

Blaze

Star

Stripe

Black

Red dun

Fleabitten gray

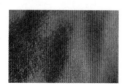

Liver chestnut

Piebald

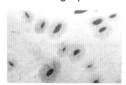

Leopard Appaloosa

Red chestnut

Skewbald

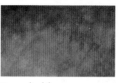

Dappled brown

Rose roan

Dappled beige dun

Cream

Dark liver

Dappled chestnut

Dappled gray

Bay

Palomino

Gray

HORSE
BREEDS

The Americas, 18

Great Britain and Ireland, 28

Europe, 36

Russia, Baltic States and
Scandinavia, 52

Australia, Asia and Africa, 60

QUARTER HORSE

Named after the quarter-mile race in 17th century Virginia and the Carolinas. It is noted for its extremely fast starts and great speed over short distances. It is an ideal ranch horse. They are the most numerous breed in the USA.

Origin USA.
Height 15–16hh.
Color Solid colors.
Physique Large build, muscular.
Character Intelligent, sensible, nimble, active.
Principal uses Riding, ranchwork, rodeos, racing.

15–16hh

SADDLEBRED

Developed as an enduring working horse, they are one of the most glamorous and loving horses in the world. The breed's gait distinguishes it from others, "slow gait", "rack", "three-gaited" and "five-gaited", were developed for long hours under saddle.

Origin USA.
Height 15–16hh.
Color Solid colors, including Palomino.
Physique Long legs, high neck and nicked and set tail.
Character Fiery, spirited, gentle.
Principal uses Show horse, jumper.

15–16hh

APPALOOSA

Bred by the American Indian tribe, the Nez Percé, from stock brought by the *conquistadores*. They have a patterned coat with six variations of mottling and spotting. They are used as competition, working, parade and display horses.

Origin USA.
Height 14–15hh
Color White pattern with spots of chestnut, brown, black.
Physique Compact, strong legs.
Character Docile, enthusiastic.
Principal uses Riding, dressage, cross-country, show jumping.

TENNESSEE WALKING HORSE

Developed by plantation owners for long hours in the saddle. They are all round riding and harness horses. They owe their existence to one stallion which was discarded because of his strange walk and founded a new breed.

Origin USA.
Height Not less than 15hh.
Color Chestnut, brown, black with white markings.
Physique Compact, well-muscled, strong legs and feet.
Character Docile, alert.
Principal uses Show ring, general riding, harness horse.

PONY OF THE AMERICAS

Bred from the Scottish Shetland Pony from Britain and the Iberian-based American Appaloosa. They have the Appaloosa coloring and patterns and the conformation of a miniature Arab/Quarter Horse cross.

Origin USA.
Height 11–13hh.
Color White pattern with spots of chestnut, brown, black.
Physique Arab-type head, strong hindquarters, clean legs.
Character Versatile, willing, gentle.
Principal uses Children's riding pony.

11–13hh

STANDARDBRED

The fastest trotting and pacing racer in the world. Bred for one purpose only, to trot or pace harnessed to an ultralight, two-wheeled racing sulky for one mile (1.6km) to a minimum standard time.

Origin USA.
Height 14–16hh.
Color Brown, black, bay with black tail and mane, chestnut.
Physique Muscular, short legs, powerful shoulders.
Character Docile, easy to handle, energetic, competitive.
Principal uses Trotting and pacing races.

14–16hh

MISSOURI FOX TROTTER

Developed by settlers who wanted a comfortable, speedy enduring horse able to cross all terrains. They have been raced but are now more of a utility, all purpose horse. They have a distinctive fox trotting gait.

Origin USA.
Height 14–16hh.
Color Chestnut, brown, pinto.
Physique Substantial, stylish horse, fine legs, strong feet.
Character Hardiness, willing to work, versatile, great stamina.
Principal uses Leisure riding, showing and endurance riding.

14–16hh

AMERICAN SHETLAND

The breed was started from Shetland Ponies imported into America. The American Shetland retains the thick Shetland mane and tail hair, but has a definite horse character and longer body and legs.

Origin USA.
Height Up to 11hh.
Color Solid colors, roan, cream and dun.
Physique Rugged, long legs, long feet.
Character Intelligent, easy to keep.
Principal uses Harness classes: sulky racing, four-wheeled buggy, driving, children's shows.

11hh

MORGAN

The most versatile of the American
breeds, an all-round riding and light
harness horse. It was the official mount
of the US Cavalry until mechanization,
and has been instrumental in founding
several other American breeds.

Origin USA.
Height 14–15hh.
Color Hay, brown, black.
Physique Broad back, muscular
hindquarters, legs set square.
Character Spirit, stamina, speed.
Principal uses All-rounder, ideal
family horse.

14–15hh

CRIOLLO

The breed's ancestors, Iberian, Barb
and Arab horses, arrived in America
300 years ago. Adaptable to the
extremes of climate, breeding stock
undergo selection tests where the
horses are marched for 470 miles
(750km) carrying 238lb (108kg).

Origin USA.
Height 14–15hh.
Color Primitive dun or brown.
Physique Stocky, strong shoulders
and legs, small feet.
Character Hardy, independent.
Principal uses Cattle horse,
endurance riding.

14–15hh

FALABELLA

Claimed to be the smallest horse in the world, the breed was founded by crossing Shetland and Thoroughbred blood. Continual breeding for smaller size has resulted in inherited and congenital weaknesses which breeders are trying to overcome.

Origin USA.
Height Not exceeding 30in (75cm).
Color Appaloosa type coloring.
Physique Horse-like proportions, not strong, small feet.
Character Quiet, friendly.
Principal uses Pets, shown in hand, pulling small vehicles.

MANGALARGA

They are descended from an Altér Real stallion and South American Criollo mares. The Mangalarga has a fifth gait called the *marcha*, which is a fast, rolling gait halfway between the trot and canter, making the breed useful for stock work.

Origin Brazil.
Height 15hh.
Color Bay, gray, chestnut, roan.
Physique Long head, powerful hindquarters, long legs.
Character Tough, hardy, cooperative.
Principal uses Stock work on ranches of Brazil.

THE AMERICAS

AZTECA

The Azteca replaces the Mexican strain of Criollo. Andalusian stallions were crossed with South American Criollo and Quarter Horse mares to produce a horse for leisure riding and competition. They have the qualities of speed, agility of the Quarter Horse, and toughness of the Criollo.

Origin Mexico.
Height 14–15hh.
Color All colors.
Physique Elegant, compact, agile.
Character Tough, hardy, stamina.
Principal uses Leisure riding and competition.

14–15hh

GALICENO

Descended from the Spanish pony, they are a popular pony for older children and adaptable for showing and competing. They have great stamina and a natural fast running walk, which is comfortable over long distances.

Origin Mexico.
Height 12–13hh.
Color All colors.
Physique Intelligent head, short back, fine legs, small feet.
Character Tough, hardy, intelligent, lovely temperament.
Principal uses Ranch work and light harness work.

12–13hh

PERUVIAN STEPPING HORSE

The blood brother of the Paso Fino, the Peruvian Stepping Horse has developed a large heart and lungs to enable it to work in an atmosphere of very low oxygen. They instinctively work on rocky ground, sliding shale, deep water and steep inclines without fear or panic.

Origin Peru.
Height 14–15hh.
Color All colors, bay or chestnut.
Physique Sure footed, strong legs.
Character Calm, enduring, willing.
Principal uses Ranching, travel, parade work, showing.

PASO FINO

The Paso Fino comes from Puerto Rico and is the best-looking of the Paso types. It is famous for its refined gaits the *paso fino*, the *paso corto* or *fino fino* and the *paso largo*. It is also a working horse and is used for transportation on coffee plantations.

Origin Puerto Rico.
Height 14–15hh.
Color All colors.
Physique Refined gaits, Arab-type head, Andalusian body.
Character Gentle temperament, easy to handle, intelligent.
Principal uses Riding, showing, display work, transportation.

POLO PONY

The Polo Pony is a *type* of pony, not a breed. They need to be tough, agile, and fast over short distances. The best polo ponies are usually regarded as the Argentinian ones; although most countries where polo is played, breed some of their own ponies.

Origin Argentina.
Height 15hh.
Color All colors.
Physique Fit, strong, natural balance, powerful hindquarters.
Character Determined, obedient.
Principal uses Polo games.

15hh

PALOMINO

The Palomino is not strictly a breed but a color. There is no actual Palomino stud book as they cannot be made to breed to color. The exception to this is in America where there is a register of color-breeds with strict requirements.

Origin USA.
Height Over 14hh.
Color Gold, light mane and tail.
Physique Riding horse type.
Character Intelligent.
Principal uses Riding, rodeos, trekking, ranchwork.

Over 14hh

PINTO

The term means horses with large patches of white and one other color on their bodies. Only in the USA is the Pinto regarded as a true breed. The Native American tribes loved these horses as their broken outline provided camouflage.

Origin USA.
Height Variable.
Color Black patches with white, white with any color except black.
Physique Depends on type.
Character Intelligent, enduring.
Principal uses Showing, ranchwork, riding.

Variable

MUSTANG

The Mustang is the feral horse of the North Americas and was used by Indian tribes. The Mustang developed toughness to cope with living wild, but few run free today. Most are enclosed on ranches, or used to breed riding and ranch horses.

Origin Western USA/ Mexico.
Height 14–15hh.
Color All colors.
Physique Lightweight, sturdy build, tough legs and feet.
Character Independent, intractable.
Principal uses Endurance riding, stockwork, riding.

14–15hh

CLYDESDALE HORSE

Originated in the Clyde Valley when Flemish stallions were mated with native mares. They were developed for carrying coal and although their use as a haulage and farm horse has decreased, their popularity as dray horses is increasing.

Origin Great Britain.
Height 16–17hh.
Color Roan, bay, brown, chestnut.
Physique Heavy build, strong, large feet, short back.
Character Calm temperament.
Principal uses Haulage, showing, competitive ploughing.

16–17hh

DALES PONY

The breed originates from the north of England. At one time, they and the Fell pony were collectively called Pennine Ponies. They are superb trotting ponies, and were used for transporting ammunition in wartime, and surface work in the mining industry.

Origin Great Britain.
Height Up to 14hh.
Color Black, brown, bays, grays.
Physique Powerful body, short legs, neat head.
Character Quiet, intelligent.
Principal uses Trekking, competition driving.

14hh

DARTMOOR PONY

The Dartmoor is a superb example of a riding pony. The habitat of the Dartmoor Pony is wild and harsh, supporting poor vegetation and scrub. The pony is tough and hardy but needs hay to survive over the winter.

Origin Great Britain.
Height Up to 12hh.
Color Bay, brown.
Physique Sturdy, strong hindquarters, slim hard legs.
Character Quiet, sensible, kind.
Principal uses Ideal children's riding pony and competitive driving.

EXMOOR PONY

One of the purest pony breeds in the world still run free on Exmoor, although most are owned by local farmers and wardens. The breed is a neighbor of the Dartmoor and is just as wild.

Origin Great Britain.
Height Up to 12hh.
Color Bay, brown, or dun.
Physique Sturdy, thickset, strong legs.
Character Willing, hard working.
Principal uses Trekking, competition driving, endurance riding.

SHETLAND PONY

Named after the islands in the far north of Scotland, the Shetland has developed due to the extreme climate. They are small, tough ponies adept at reducing heat loss but lose type when exported to breed elsewhere in the world.

Origin Great Britain.
Height 40in (100cm).
Color All colors.
Physique Small head, deep thick-set body, short legs small open feet.
Character Headstrong.
Principal uses Children's riding pony, harness and driving events.

40in

FELL PONY

Related to the Dales Pony, the Fell is smaller and purer blood. They are true mountain and moorland ponies, still bred and running free on the hills. They were used for sheep herding, trotting-racing and as pack ponies.

Origin Great Britain.
Height Up to 14hh.
Color Black, brown, bay, gray.
Physique Long neck, muscular body, strong legs.
Character Friendly, willing, determined nature.
Principal uses Children's riding pony, harness, herding, trekking.

14hh

SHIRE HORSE

The Shires are the tallest horses in the world. They were developed in the 19th century to meet the demand for a stronger animal to pull the heavier farm machinery and transportation vehicles.

Origin Great Britain.
Height 17–18hh.
Color Bay with dapples, brown, black with white on face and legs.
Physique Dense muscular body, long legs, wide chest.
Character Docile, patient, gentle.
Principal uses Dray, working, ploughing matches, pulling contests.

17–18hh

HACKNEY HORSE

Used in the Middle Ages, they were developed as a fast means of transport on the expanding road network. They can be traced back to the Yorkshire and Norfolk trotters and may descend from Danish horses.

Origin Great Britain.
Height Up to 12–15hh.
Color Bay, brown, black.
Physique Small head, compact body, short legs, high set tail.
Character Fiery, fast, alert.
Principal uses Show ring, carriage driving and show jumping.

12–15hh

HIGHLAND PONY

This native Scottish pony has a good temperament having lived in close contact with people for hundreds of years. There have been two strains: the smaller Western Isles type, and the Garron from the mainland. Cross breeding has now more or less eliminated these distinctions.

Origin Great Britain.
Height 14hh.
Color Range of shades of dun.
Physique Deep body, short legs.
Character Trusting, cooperative.
Principal uses Crofting, forestry, deer ponies, trekking, pets.

14hh

THOROUGHBRED

Although bred purely for racing by British royalty, the popularity of the sport has led to the spread of Thoroughbred racing and breeding worldwide. Imported Arab stallions in England were mixed with more Oriental blood to produce a larger, faster, horse with longer stride.

Origin Great Britain.
Height 15–16hh.
Color Solid colors.
Physique Elegant, refined, quality.
Character Fast, highly strung.
Principal uses Racing, hurdles, steeplechase, showing, competition.

15–16hh

NEW FOREST PONY

The largest and least hardy of Britain's ponies, they have traditionally grazed on open scrubland and been used for farming and transport. When the New Forest is crossed with Thoroughbred or Arab stallions, they produce good performance horses.

Origin Great Britain.
Height 12–14hh.
Color Any colors.
Physique Short back with deep girth, nimble footed, strong.
Character Calm, intelligent.
Principal uses Riding, trekking, forest rides.

12–14hh

SUFFOLK PUNCH

A small and heavy horse, the Suffolk was developed by crossing Flanders horses with heavy mares from East Anglia. They met a need for smaller, agile, heavy horses required around towns and cities. The Suffolk is renowned for working long hours, needing little rest.

Origin Great Britain.
Height 15–16hh.
Color Shades of chestnut.
Physique Large head, massive shoulders, lean legs.
Character Willing workers, gentle.
Principal uses Showing, dray work.

15–16hh

WELSH COB

The Welsh Cobs have been in use for centuries for farming, herding sheep under saddle, and taking the family to chapel in a cart. Welsh Cob stallions are renowned for their fire and personality, unique to their breed.

Origin Great Britain.
Height 15hh.
Color All colors.
Physique Compact, good head, strong shoulders, deep back.
Character Stylish, gentle.
Principal uses Competitive driving, jumping, cross-country, show jumping.

15hh

ANGLO-ARAB

A combination of two breeds, the Arab and an English breed of Thoroughbred. It is common to mate an Arab stallion with a Thoroughbred mare, but the reverse may also occur. They make superb riding horses.

Origin Great Britain.
Height 14–16hh.
Color Any parent color.
Physique Deep chest, short back, well-proportioned hindquarters.
Character Spirited, "thinkers", affectionate, courageous.
Principal uses Competitions, dressage, eventing, show jumping.

14–16hh

IRISH DRAFT

The breed was developed by farmers as a working horse and for hunting and riding. Irish Draft crossed with a suitable Thoroughbred produce superb horses capable of jumping and crossing any country when hunting or in competition.

Origin Ireland.
Height 15–17hh.
Color Solid colors, black is rare.
Physique Long powerful body, strong legs, large round feet.
Character Spirited, amenable.
Principal uses Riding horse, hunter, breeding stock.

CONNEMARA

The Connemara is a native breed, descended from the Irish Hobbye which had great speed, stamina, agility and reliability. They are a good cross with Thoroughbreds producing performance horses for riding and jumping.

Origin Ireland.
Height 13–14hh.
Color Mainly gray, solid colors.
Physique Deep compact body on short legs, intelligent looking.
Character Tough, hardy docile.
Principal uses Riding pony, hunter, hack, trekking mount.

COB

The term cob refers to a distinct type of strong, stocky horse. Only the Welsh Cob is classified as a breed. They are ideal for elderly and nervous riders and are also immensely strong and can carry a heavy rider all day.

Origin Great Britain.
Height 15hh.
Color All colors.
Physique Stocky, compact, short back, short strong legs.
Character Intelligent, obedient, placid.
Principal uses Riding, hunting.

15hh

HUNTER

The term hunter refers to a horse that is suited to carrying a rider behind foxhounds safely, sensibly, for a season's hunting. They provide a mount with a calm temperament, surefootedness, lots of stamina and a good instinct for self preservation.

Origin Great Britain.
Height 14–16hh.
Color Solid colors with white.
Physique Strong back, powerful hindquarters, long hard legs.
Character Obedient, controllable.
Principal uses Showing, hunting.

14–16hh

HACK

The term hack comes from the word hackney which in medieval times referred to a hired horse of poor quality. The modern hack however, is based on the Thoroughbred and is known for its conformation, presence, good manners and quality of ride.

Origin Great Britain.
Height 14–15hh.
Color Solid colors with white.
Physique Thoroughbred type with attractive head.
Character Obedient, responsive, comfortable.
Principal uses Riding, showing.

14–15hh

RIDING PONY

The riding pony type, has been developed to provide a mount that is particularly suitable for children. Thoroughbred blood has been infused, to produce ponies that are athletic, elegant and gentle in addition to their traditional sturdiness.

Origin Great Britain.
Height Under 14.2hh.
Color All colors.
Physique Broad body, sturdy.
Character Intelligent, good natured.
Principal uses Children's riding, show jumping.

14.2hh

SELLE FRANÇAIS

The Selle Français exhibits considerable variety of type within its breed.
They resemble a middleweight
Thoroughbred of good
conformation and are
excellent performance horses.

Origin France.
Height 15–16hh.
Color Chestnut, bay, gray.
Physique Short back,
powerful hindquarters, well-set head.
Character Variable, common sense.
Principal uses Competitions,
leisure/riding horse, show jumping.

15–16hh

FRENCH TROTTER

The sport of trotting is popular in
France, both in harness and under
saddle and the French Trotters have
been bred for speed. Horses which
do not prove themselves at racing
do well at jumping and riding.

Origin France.
Height 16hh.
Color Chestnut, bay, brown.
Physique Strong, straight shoulders,
short back, well-muscled hindquarters,
long hard legs.
Character Good temperament.
Principal uses Trotting, racing in
saddle and under harness.

16hh

CAMARGUE PONY

These horses graze on coastal grass up to their knees in salt water. They are annually rounded up to select riding horses, the sub-standard colts and stallions are culled to improve the breed.

Origin France.
Height 13–14hh.
Color White-gray, bay and brown.
Physique Oriental head, short back, fine legs, large feet.
Character Once broken in, docile and willing, spirited.
Principal uses Herding black bulls, trekking mounts.

13–14hh

FRENCH ANGLO-ARAB

One of the best riding horses in the world. They are bred from Anglo-Arab, Thoroughbred and Arab blood. The horses must have at least 25 percent Arab blood and the absence of any other than Arab and Thoroughbred blood for at least six years.

Origin France.
Height 15–16hh.
Color Chestnut, all colors
Physique Deep chest, well-proportioned hindquarters, long legs.
Character Intelligent, good natured.
Principal uses Show jumping, dressage, endurance riding.

15–16hh

E
U
R
O
P
E

FRIESIAN

One of the oldest European horse breeds, the Friesian comes from Holland where it is used as a working horse. It has been used in the formation of Britain's Fell and Dales Ponies and influenced trotting breeds throughout the world.

Origin Holland.
Height 15hh.
Color Black.
Physique Long head, strong compact body, short legs.
Character Quiet, hard working.
Principal uses Driving, riding, all-round workhorse.

15hh

GELDERLANDER

Created by farmers who wanted to produce horses for their own use as well as to sell. They are now a recognizable, top class light carriage and saddle horse and have been used by several royal houses of Europe.

Origin Holland.
Height 15–16hh.
Color Solid colors, chestnut.
Physique Plain head, deep shoulders, compact body, powerful hindquarters, short legs.
Character Quiet, good natured.
Principal uses Riding, driving, carriage horse.

15–16hh

DUTCH DRAFT

These are the heaviest draft horses for their height and are probably descended from medieval knight's horses crossed with Brabant and the Belgian Ardennais. Despite their massive size, they are docile and active.

Origin Holland.
Height 17hh.
Color Chestnut, bay, gray, black.
Physique Heavy and massive, very strong, pillar like legs,
Character Docile, willing, intelligent.
Principal uses Farm work, heavy draft work, pulling brewer's drays.

DUTCH WARMBLOOD

A new breed, the Dutch Warmblood is one of the most successful, popular, and sought-after competition and riding horses in the world. A product of the 20th century, its foundation is the Gelderlander and the Groningen as well as other European blood.

Origin Holland.
Height 16hh.
Color Bay, brown, chestnut.
Physique Long, flowing gaits.
Character Quiet, willing, intelligent, spirited.
Principal uses Showing, dressage, general riding horse, carriage driving.

PERCHERON

The most famous of the French draft horses they were bred to carry armored knights into battle. They are heavier and "chunkier" than the Clydesdale, but just as elegant and active. They are resistant to most types of weather conditions and are adaptable to new climates.

Origin France.
Height 15–17hh.
Color Gray or black.
Physique Elegant head, short legs.
Character Intelligent, good natured.
Principal uses Draft, agriculture. logging, breeding.

15–17hh

BRABANT

Also known as the Belgian Heavy Draft, the Brabant has influenced almost every other breed in the world. It is one of the strongest of the heavy breeds and has been used to improve other breeds of heavy horse.

Origin Belgium.
Height 14hh.
Color Red roan, bay, brown, dun.
Physique Square head, compact body, massive hindquarters.
Character Docile, hard working, good natured, active.
Principal uses Draft and farm work.

14hh

SALERNO

Developed from the Neapolitan, the Salerno was favored by royalty. They later became cavalry mounts and with the introduction of Thoroughbred and Arab blood, they are excellent carriage horses and show jumpers.

Origin Italy.
Height 16hh.
Color Any solid color.
Physique Refined head, prominent withers, strong sloping hindquarters.
Character Intelligent, responsive.

16hh

ITALIAN HEAVY DRAFT

Bred from several different blood lines, the Italian Heavy Draft is a distinctive breed. The Italians did not want to breed massive horses, eventually settling for a cross with the Postier-Breton for a smaller, lighter, more active horse.

Origin Italy.
Height 14–16hh.
Color Chestnut, flaxen mane, forelock and tail.
Physique Powerful shoulders, robust body, muscular legs.
Character Friendly, calm, energetic.
Principal uses Farm work.

14–16hh

HAFLINGER

Modern Haflingers descend from an Arab stallion introduced in 1868 to upgrade the coarse stock. Regarded as an Austrian breed, it has an Italian counterpart, the Avelignese which is slightly bigger. They are popular European ponies.

Origin Austria.
Height 14hh.
Color Chestnut, flaxen mane/tail.
Physique Long back, well-muscled hindquarters, short legs.
Character Docile, hard working.
Principal uses Mountain pony, driving packhorse, riding.

14hh

NORIKER

An ancient breed, the Noriker is founded on various heavy breeds, introduced by the Romans. They have been developed to suit agricultural and forestry work in the harsh climates of mountainous terrain.

Origin Austria.
Height 15–16hh.
Color Bay, chestnut, roan, spotted.
Physique Well-muscled shoulders, sturdy legs, sure-footed.
Character Strong, calm, quiet.
Principal uses Farming, forestry, transportation.

15–16hh

LIPPIZANER

One of the world's most famous breeds, from the Spanish Riding School of Vienna renowned for their displays of high-school dressage.
They are used as carriage horses in Hungary and circuses around the world.

Origin Austria.
Height 15–16hh.
Color Gray.
Physique Compact body, powerful hindquarters, clean legs, agile.
Character Obedient, intelligent, proud.
Principal uses *Haute Ecole.*

15–16hh

KLADRUBER

The Kladruber comes from the world's oldest operational stud in Kladruby. They were originally bred as ceremonial coach horses for Emperor Maximillian II in 1597. Today's smaller animals are excellent riding and draft horses.

Origin Czech Republic.
Height 16–17hh.
Color Gray or black.
Physique Andalusian type, long body and rounded hindquarters.
Character Proud, obedient, intelligent, good natured.
Principal uses Driving, riding.

16–17hh

WIELKOPOLSKI

The Wielkopolski is descended from the remaining stock at the Trakehnen stud at the end of World War II. They became the foundation stock for the Masuren and the Poznan which were then combined to form the Wielkopolski.

Origin Poland.
Height 16hh.
Color All solid colors.
Physique Small head, deep girth, fine legs, medium length back.
Character Gentle, intelligent.
Principal uses Riding, light draft work.

EAST FRIESIAN

The East Friesian has developed alongside its blood brother, the Oldenburg, and been bred with Arabs and Hanoverians to produce a lighter, more compact horse, suited to competitions.

Origin Germany.
Height 16–17hh.
Color Any solid color.
Physique Muscular chest and body, strong hindquarters, short legs.
Character Bold, sensible.
Principal uses Riding, competition, driving.

SHAGYA ARAB

Named after the gray Arab which sired the breed, the Shagya was developed by crossing Arabs and native stock to produce a robust cavalry mount and light carriage horse. They are of the highest quality but not well-known outside their home country.

Origin Hungary.
Height 14–15hh.
Color Satiny, gray coat.
Physique Arab-type, but robust.
Character Intelligent, hardy.
Principal uses Riding, cavalry, driving.

TRAKEHNER

The Trakehnen stud developed the Trakehner using local Schwieken horses. At the end of World War II, 700 Trakehners trekked west with refugees and these horses were used to re-establish the breed in Germany.

Origin Poland/Germany.
Height 16hh.
Color Any solid color, usually dark.
Physique Elegant head, deep chest, strong back, slender legs.
Character Spirited, courageous, versatile, tractable.
Principal uses Riding, competition.

HANOVERIAN

The breed has altered from its origins to suit different requirements. The farm horse was adapted to the needs of the army and further developed for farming and riding. After World War II, breeders have been aiming at world-class competition horses.

Origin Germany.
Height 15–17hh.
Color All solid colors.
Physique Variable, but a compact, powerful body on short strong legs.
Character Intelligent, sensible, bold.
Principal uses Riding, competition.

15–17hh

SCHLESWIG HEAVY DRAFT

The Schleswig was developed during the 19th century specifically to meet the demand for horses capable of heavy agricultural work. It has the blood of other heavy horses including the Jutland, a Danish war-horse.

Origin Germany.
Height 15–16hh.
Color Usually chestnut with flaxen mane and tail.
Physique Large head, deep girth, long body on short muscular legs.
Character Kind and willing.
Principal uses Draft.

15–16hh

HOLSTEIN

The Holstein is known to have lived in the marshlands of Schleswig-Holstein in the 14th century, and was originally a heavy, powerful horse. Since the 19th century, it has been successively bred with lighter, more refined breeds.

Origin Germany.
Height 16–17hh.
Color Most solid colors.
Physique Elegant head, strong hindquarters, short legs.
Character Intelligent, versatile.
Principal uses Riding, competition.

16-17hh

OLDENBURG

The Oldenburg was ousted as a working horse after World War II, so breeders lightened their horse for riding. Further Thoroughbred blood was introduced, and they are now used for carriage work and competitive riding.

Origin Germany
Height 16–17hh.
Color Black, brown, bay.
Physique Muscular chest and body, strong hindquarters, short legs.
Character Bold, sensible.
Principal uses Riding, competition, driving.

16-17hh

FURIOSO

One of Hungary's high-quality half-breeds, they excel as a harness horse and are in demand all over the world for competition driving. A Furioso/North Star cross, the Mozohegyes, is fast becoming Hungary's top sports horse.

Origin Hungary.
Height 16hh.
Color Dark, with white markings.
Physique Powerful shoulders, strong back, powerful hindquarters.
Character Tractable, intelligent.
Principal uses Riding, competition, steeple-chasing, driving.

16hh

ANDALUSIAN

This elegant horse has been used in the founding of other breeds including the Lippizaner, Peruvian Stepping Horse and the Paso Fino. They are much sought after and excel at high-school work.

Origin Spain.
Height 15–16hh.
Color Usually gray.
Physique Deep short body, powerful round hindquarters, strong legs.
Character Docile, willing, proud, affectionate.
Principal uses High-school dressage, parades, bull-fighting.

15–16hh

ALTÉR REAL

The national horse of Portugal is closely related to its neighbor, the Andalusian, and was bred from them during the 18th century when the fashion was for high-school dressage competitions.

Origin Portugal.
Height 15–16hh.
Color Bay, brown, gray.
Physique Strong shoulders, short body, powerful hindquarters, hard legs.
Character Intelligent, highly strung.
Principal uses Riding, high-school dressage.

15–16hh

LUSITANO

Once primarily a cavalry horse, the Lusitano was used by farmers for their strength. Best known as the mounts of bull-fighters, they are renowned for their agility, speed, obedience and training.

Origin Portugal.
Height 15–16hh.
Color Usually gray.
Physique Small head, compact body, powerful hindquarters, long fine legs, abundant mane and tail.
Character Intelligent, responsive, brave.
Principal uses Riding, bull-fighting.

15–16hh

ORLOV TROTTER

The best known of the Russian horse breeds, the Orlov was developed in the 18th century when trotting races were very popular. They have been recently crossed with the Standardbred to produce the Russian Trotter.

Origin Russia.
Height 15–17hh.
Color Gray or black.
Physique Broad chest, long back, powerful loins, fine hard legs.
Character Active, bold.
Principal Uses Trotting, driving, riding.

15–17hh

DON

The Don's toughness, stamina and ability to cope with vicious weather, led it to be used as the Cossack's mount. Persian Arab and other Oriental blood has been introduced to heighten, refine and correct the Don's physique.

Origin Russian steppes.
Height 15–16hh.
Color Chestnut, bay, gray.
Physique Long neck, long back, strong hindquarters, long hard legs.
Character Calm, reliable, independent.
Principal uses Riding, long-distance riding/racing, breeding.

15–16hh

BUDYONNY

Created after the Russian Revolution, the Budyonny was bred to produce a perfect cavalry horse for the military. Thoroughbred stallions on Don mares proved successful. Large herds still run free.

Origin Russia.
Height 15–16hh.
Color Chestnut, bay with a sheen.
Physique Small head, strong compact body, fine hard legs.
Character Spirited, patient, kind, courageous.
Principal uses Flat-racing, competition, steeple-chase.

15–16hh

KABARDIN

An adaptable animal, the Kabardin can live at sea-level or in the mountains. It is a descendant of the Tarpan and remained unchanged until the Russian Revolution, when Oriental blood was introduced to improve its height and riding work.

Origin Russia.
Height 14–15hh.
Color Bay, brown, black.
Physique Long head, long ears, long back.
Character Intelligent, sensible.
Principal uses Transportation, sports, breeding.

14–15hh

TERSKY

There are three types of Tersky and all are excellent performance horses. They were bred for steeple-chasing but are usually raced on the flat against other Arabs. They are popular in dressage and the circus ring.

Origin Russia.
Height 15hh.
Color Usually gray.
Physique Deep chest, muscular hindquarters, fine hard legs.
Character Gentle, intelligent.
Principal uses Flat-racing, competition, circus.

15hh

KARABAKH

The Karabakh look like Arabs as both come from the same genetic type. They have existed since the 4th century and remain a popular riding mount. As it has been mixed with Persian, Turkmene and Arab blood, it is said that there are no pure Karabakh left.

Origin Azerbaijan.
Height 14hh.
Color Dun, bay or chestnut.
Physique Strong compact body, fine legs, powerful hindquarters.
Character Quick-witted, calm, robust.
Principal uses Riding, racing.

14hh

UKRAINIAN RIDING HORSE

Founded by crossing several large breeds with native mares, to produce a good sporting horse for high-class riding and competitions. They have been bred for temperament and are quality warmbloods.

Origin Ukraine.
Height 16hh.
Color Chestnut, bay, black.
Physique Elegant, refined.
Character Obliging, willing, kind-natured.
Principal uses High-class competition, riding, light harness.

LATVIAN

There are three types of Latvian; the heavy, Latvian Draft; the standard, Latvian Harness Horse; the lighter, Latvian Riding Horse. Scandinavian blood was introduced to increase substance and strength.

Origin Latvia.
Height 16hh.
Color Black, brown, bay, chestnut.
Physique Strong, great stamina.
Character Relaxed, quiet.
Principal uses Heavy farm work or competition riding.

SWEDISH WARMBLOOD

Developed as a cavalry horse, the
Swedish Warmblood is in demand for
show-jumping, eventing and dressage.
They are one of the most successful
competition horses in the world and
their quality is rigorously monitored.

Origin Sweden.
Height 16–17hh.
Color Solid colors.
Physique Elegant, deep body, fine
legs, rounded hindquarters.
Character Sensible, intelligent.
Principal uses Riding, driving,
competition.

16–17hh

GOTLAND

A descendant of the Tarpan, the
Gotland pony has run wild on the
Swedish island since pre-historic times.
They were used for farming and trans-
portation but their popularity abroad
led to their depletion in numbers.

Origin Sweden.
Height 12–13hh.
Color Black, bay.
Physique Well muscled, fine legs.
Character Independent, tractable,
willing.
Principal uses Trotting races, riding,
light harness.

12–13hh

NORTHLANDS

Little known outside Norway, the Northlands closely resembles the Scottish Shetland Pony. They were used and bred by farmers with little selection policy. Numbers declined in the 1920s but one fine stallion brought them back from certain extinction.

Origin Norway.
Height 13–14hh.
Color Chestnut, gray, bay, brown.
Physique Strong legs, large head, small tough feet.
Character Quiet natured, energetic.
Principal uses Children's riding pony, farm work.

13–14hh

DØLE-GUDBRANDSDAL

The Døle and the Gudbrandsdal were originally separate breeds which have amalgamated. They account for almost two thirds of Norway's horse population. They have had Thoroughbred and Arab blood introduced, to produce an offshoot, the Døle Trotter (pictured).

Origin Norway.
Height 13–14hh.
Color Black, brown.
Physique Powerful body, short legs.
Character Kind, patient.
Principal uses Farm work, forestry, trotting races.

13–14hh

FJORD

The Fjord's color, marking and ancient mane trimming are unique in the equine world. The Fjord has been bred into the Highland Pony and the Icelandic Pony.

Origin Norway.
Height 13-14hh.
Color Distinctive yellow or dun.
Physique Powerful body, short legs, coarse mane in three layers.
Character Strong willed, tractable.
Principal uses Farm work, driving, mountain work, packhorse.

13-14hh

FREDRIKSBORG

One of the original *Haute Ecole* horses, the Fredriksborg was bred for speed and stamina. They were used as an officer's charger and as carriage horses for state occasions. Few of the old types of Fredriksborg remain and new blood has been introduced to breed up the numbers.

Origin Denmark.
Height 15–16hh.
Color Chestnut.
Physique Deep chest, long body, strong legs.
Character Good tempered, tractable.
Principal uses Riding, driving.

15-16hh

KNABSTRUP

The Knabstrup was a victim of breeding almost entirely for color and the breed deteriorated. The introduction of Thoroughbred blood has resulted in a much improved animal, distinctive for its spotted coat.

Origin Denmark.
Height 15hh.
Color Spotted; Appaloosa patterns.
Physique Varies, similar to Fredriksborg but lighter.
Character Intelligent, tractable.
Principal uses Riding, circus.

ICELANDIC

There are several variations of Icelandic but all share great stamina, strength and sure-footedness. Their unusual gaits are the amble, a running walk and a rapid amble. The Icelandic lives in a half wild state, surviving the harsh winters by foraging.

Origin Iceland.
Height 12–13hh.
Color Most colors.
Physique Large head, compact body, strong legs, large feet.
Character Intelligent, tractable.
Principal uses Riding, circus.

ARAB

The Arab has greatly influenced the breeding of horses and ponies throughout the world, more than any other, as it breeds true to type. They are famous for their stamina and are in much demand as competition endurance horses.

Origin Arabia.
Height 14hh.
Color Chestnut, bay, gray.
Physique Small head, strong hindquarters, hard clean legs.
Character Brave, fiery, intelligent, enduring.
Principal uses Riding, breeding.

14hh

CASPIAN

Believed to be extinct, a herd of 40 Caspian horses was discovered on the shores of the Caspian Sea, in 1965, and were brought to Britain. These small horses are now increasing in numbers at studs throughout the world.

Origin Iran.
Height 10–12hh.
Color Chestnut, bay, gray.
Physique Arab-type head, narrow body, short back, fine legs.
Character Gentle, quick witted, tractable.
Principal uses Riding, driving.

10–12hh

AKHAL-TEKÉ

The descendant of the Turkmene, the Akhal-Teké has evolved to be one of the most hardy and enduring horses. They are desert horses and still run in managed herds, but need heavy covers to protect their fine skin from the desert sun and bitter nights.

Origin Turkmenistan.
Height 14–15hh.
Color Chestnut, bay.
Physique Small head, long back, shallow body, long legs.
Character Obstinate, difficult to handle.
Principal uses Riding, competition.

14–15hh

PRZEWALSKI'S HORSE

Discovered by a Polish explorer, the Przewalski had been hunted almost to extinction. There have been no wild horses seen since 1970 and animals are now being bred from captive stock, in order to reintroduce the breed.

Origin Mongolia.
Height 12–14hh.
Color Yellow dun.
Physique Stocky, long back, fine legs, tough feet.
Character Ferocious temperament, untamed, courageous.
Principal uses Breeding.

12–14hh

BARB

An old Oriental-type breed, the Barb has helped to found other breeds. They are tough, enduring, fast and responsive and are the mount of the Bedouin people. Few pure-bred Barbs are left as Arab blood has been introduced to make them easier to train.

Origin North Africa.
Height 14–15hh.
Color Bay, chestnut, black, gray.
Physique Large head, long back, long fine legs.
Character Quick tempered, courageous.
Principal uses Riding, cross-breeding.

14–15hh

JAVA PONY

The Java Pony has had the benefit of Arab blood which makes it bigger and stronger than other ponies in Indonesia. It is a widespread "taxi" pony on Java and is also used for riding and other light draft work.

Origin Indonesia.
Height 12hh.
Color Most colors.
Physique Slightly built, strong.
Character Willing.
Principal uses Driving, all-round work pony.

12hh

AUSTRALIAN STOCK HORSE

Known until 1971 as the Waler, this hardy, agile horse was worked on cattle stations. Numbers declined after World War II and new blood was indiscriminately introduced. Arab and Thoroughbred blood has now been added to improve the horse.

Origin Australia.
Height 16hh.
Color All colors.
Physique Thoroughbred type, strong back and hindquarters.
Character Versatile, reliable worker.
Principal uses Herding, rodeos, riding, competition.

16hh

AUSTRALIAN PONY

Founded by crossing Arab with Welsh Mountain Pony, the Australian Pony is an excellent riding pony, refined yet not too light. They have a good temperament and are easy for children to ride and care for.

Origin Australia.
Height 12–14hh.
Color All colors.
Physique Arab-like head, short back, short legs with hard feet.
Character Lively, intelligent.
Principal uses Children's riding pony.

12–14hh

Index

Akhal-Teké 61
Alter Real 51
American Shetland 21
Andalusian 50
Anglo-Arab 34
Appaloosa 19
Arab 60
Australian Pony 63
Australian Stock Horse 63
Azteca 24

Barb 62
Brabant 42
Budyonny 53

Camargue 39
Caspian 60
Clydesdale Horse 28
Cob 36
Connemara 35
Criollo 22

Dartmoor Pony 29
Dales Pony 28
Døle 57
Don 52
Dutch Draft 41
Dutch Warmblood 41

East Friesian 46
Exmoor Pony 29

Falabella 23
Fell Pony 30
Fjord 58
Fredriksborg 58
Friesian 40

French Anglo-Arab 39
French Trotter 38
Furioso 50

Galiceno 24
Gelderlander 40
Gotland 56

Hack 37
Hackney Horse 31
Haflinger 44
Hanoverian 48
Highland Pony 32
Holstein 49
Hunter 36

Icelandic 59
Italian Heavy Draft 43
Irish Draft 35

Java Pony 62

Kabardin 53
Karabakh 54
Kladruber 45
Knabstrup 59

Latvian 55
Lippizaner 45
Lusitano 51

Mangalarga 23
Missouri Fox Trotter 21
Morgan 22
Mustang 77

New Forest Pony 33
Noriker 44
Northlands 56

Oldenberg 49
Orlov Trotter 52

Palomino 26
Paso Fino 25
Percheron 42
Peruvian Stepping Horse 25
Pinto 27
Polo Pony 26
Pony of Americas 20
Przewalski's Horse 61

Quarter Horse 18

Riding Pony 37

Saddlebred 18
Salerno 43
Schleswig Heavy Draft 48
Selle Français 38
Shagya Arab 47
Shetland Pony 30
Shire Horse 31
Standardbred 20
Suffolk Punch 33
Swedish Warmblood 56

Tennessee Walking Horse 19
Tersky 54
Thoroughbred 32
Trakehner 47

Ukrainian Riding Horse 55

Welsh Cob 34
Wielkopolski Horse 46

INDEX